The LOUIS ARMSTRONG
ARMSTRONG
You Never Knew

BY JAMES LINCOLN COLLIER

Children's Press®
A Division of Scholastic Inc.
New York Toronto London Auckland Sydney
Mexico City New Delhi Hong Kong
Danbury, Connecticut

Library of Congress Cataloging-in-Publication Data

Collier, James Lincoln, 1928-
  The Louis Armstrong you never knew / James Lincoln Collier.
      p. cm.
  Includes bibliographical references (p.   ) and index.
  ISBN 0-516-24429-9
  1. Armstrong, Louis, 1901-1971—Juvenile literature. 2. Jazz musicians—
United States—Biography—Juvenile literature. 3. African American jazz
musicians—Biography—Juvenile literature. I. Title.
  ML3930.A75C68 2004
  781.65'092—dc22

                                    2003028307

Illustrations by Greg Copeland
Book design by A. Natacha Pimentel C.

Photographs © 2004: AP/Wide World Photos/Kenneth Lambert: 27; Cor-
bis Images: 72, 75 (Bettmann), 8, 9; Frank Driggs Collection: cover, 15, 25,
34, 38, 49, 50, 55, 60, 62, 76 top, 76 bottom, 76 center; Hogan Jazz
Archive/Tulane University: 18, 20, 23, 36, 11, 14, 30; Hulton l Archive/Getty
Images: 41, 42, 44 (Frank Driggs Collection), 65 (Museum of the City of
New York), 28 (P.L. Sperr), 4, 52, 63, 66, 70; Time Life Pictures/Getty
Images: 69.

CONTENTS

Chapter 1

THE WAIF

FEW PEOPLE HAVE EVER RISEN AS FAR in life as Louis Armstrong did. He started at the very bottom of American society. It was hardly possible to begin life in worse conditions. By the time he was sixty he was one of the most famous entertainers in the world, and probably the best-known black person anywhere. In his time, perhaps only the Beatles and Elvis Presley were more celebrated performers. In 1964 his recording of "Hello, Dolly" was such a hit that it bumped one of the Beatles' most famous records off the top spot on the charts.

A classic photograph of Louis Armstrong with his trumpet, taken in 1965. By this time his lips were damaged, but he still played as much as he could.

Nobody who had known Louis Armstrong as a child would have in their wildest dreams imagined that he would have such enormous success, for he grew up with almost nothing. Louis's father disowned him when Louis was a little boy and would not help him in any way. At times the family was so poor that Louis had to pick through garbage cans looking for supper. He didn't own a pair of shoes until he was a teenager. His "wardrobe" usually consisted of a pair of ill-fitting pants and a couple of shirts. He didn't have a bath in a real bathtub until he was a grownup, but washed in a tub of water heated on the stove. Birthday presents for Louis were rare. And not only did he not have Christmas presents, he didn't even celebrate Christmas.

Years later, when he was a famous bandleader, he happened to be on the road on Christmas Eve. To please him, his wife brought into the hotel room a little Christmas tree, which she decorated with a few lights. When Louis got back to the hotel from playing his "gig," as musicians call their performance, he was happy to see the little tree.

Eventually they went to bed. His wife recalled, "Louis was still laying up in the bed watching the tree, his eyes just like a baby's eyes would watch something." Then it was time to go to sleep. Louis's wife said she would turn off the lights on the tree. Louis said, "No, don't turn them out. I have to just keep looking at it. You know, that's the first tree I ever had." He was forty years old.

To understand the extraordinary career of Louis Armstrong we have to know something about the city of New Orleans, where he grew up, and the jazz that was growing up with him. New Orleans, Louisiana, is in the Deep South. In Louis Armstrong's time that meant that African Americans were segregated—shut out of many of the things that whites enjoyed. Black children could not go to school with whites, but went to segregated schools, often in rundown buildings with poor equipment and out-of-date textbooks. Blacks could only eat in their own restaurants and stay in their own hotels. In railroad and bus stations they had separate waiting rooms from whites.

Canal Street in New Orleans was the dividing line between the French Quarter and the uptown area where Louis grew up. Trolley cars like these are still used in the city.

When they rode on buses and streetcars around cities, they could not take seats among white riders, but had to sit in the back.

In most cases African-American children could not expect to grow up to go to college and become doctors, lawyers, officials in government, or executives in big businesses. It is true that a small percentage of blacks did go to college, especially to all-black colleges like the famous Howard University in Washington, D.C. Such people might become professional or business people catering to blacks, but that was only a small number. Most blacks could expect to work only at the hardest, lowest-paying jobs. In New Orleans that often meant working as a washerwoman or as a stevedore on the docks, carrying boxes and bags in and out of the holds of ships.

Many New Orleans' blacks worked on the docks, loading and unloading riverboats and sea-going ships. The jobs were very hard and low-paying. Here workers, called stevedores, load a riverboat in 1901, the year Louis was born.

Even worse, when Armstrong was a boy, blacks were sometimes killed by white mobs for no reason. This was called a lynching. Sometimes the lynching was for a crime the black person was believed to have committed, but often it was because the black had spoken out too freely to a white person or was working to get justice for African Americans. As a boy Louis knew that he had to act very respectfully toward all whites, or he might get a beating. He was born into a very hard world.

And yet, it was not all pain and drudgery. Black children managed to enjoy themselves, as kids always do. Particularly important to the people of New Orleans, both black and white, was music. When Louis Armstrong was a boy, movies were only just getting started and were rough, short, and without sound. There was no television or radio. Recordings existed, but they, too, were crude, and record players were too expensive for ordinary people, much less poor ones, to own. Music was a big part of entertainment, and of course it was all live. As a result there were bands, large and small. Any kind of social club had a marching band for the many parades. There were countless dance bands, because people went out dancing whenever they could. There were symphony orchestras and operas. Even the smallest restaurants had at least a piano player.

The bigger restaurants usually had a trio or quartet, often using guitars and violins. Bands played to advertise dances, sales, and sports events. The band would travel around New Orleans playing from the back of a truck or a horse-drawn wagon, which carried a big sign giving the time and place of the dance or sale. There were usually bands at boxing matches and baseball games too.

Dances, sporting events, and sales were often advertised on wagons that rumbled through the streets of New Orleans. Sometimes bands played on these wagons to attract attention. This wagon has a sign advertising a dance at Jackson Hall, a popular dance club.

Guitarist Danny Barker, who was born in New Orleans a few years after Louis, wrote:

> *One of my pleasantest memories as a kid growing up in New Orleans was how a bunch of us kids, playing, would suddenly hear sounds. . . . The sounds of men playing would be so clear, but we wouldn't be sure where they were coming from. So we'd start trotting, start running—"It's this way! It's that way!" . . . that music could come on you any time like that. The city was full of the sounds of music.*

African-American kids learned early that they might have trouble becoming doctors or lawyers, but nothing could stop them from playing music.

There is some mystery about when Louis Armstrong was born. He always said that he was born on July 4, 1900. However, some people who knew him said he was older. His baptismal certificate states that he was born on August 4, 1901. That is probably correct, but questions remain.

Not only do we not know the date of Louis's birth, but we also can't be sure of where he was living during the time he was growing up, for he told different stories at various times. However, we do know that he rarely saw his father during his early years. For most of this part of his childhood he lived with his grandmother in a one-room cabin. The house had no electricity or running water. Water came from a pump in the yard.

The light colored building in the rear was the place where Louis Armstrong was born. The house was about the size of a big living room. It was unheated, and the water came from an outside pump nearby.

Louis's grandmother earned her living washing clothes for other people. Sometimes she went to their houses to do the laundry, sometimes she brought it home and washed it in a big tub in the yard. Many times Louis went along with her and helped as much as a little boy could. Louis's grandmother was strict with him. She saw to it that he went to church regularly, as well as to Sunday school. Even though she was strict, Louis knew that she took good care of him, and he loved her.

Then when he was five or six he moved in with his mother. He said later, "She was a stocky woman— dark, lovely expression, beautiful soul." Her name was Mary Ann, but everybody called her Mayann. She was lively and well liked in the neighborhood.

When Louis moved in with his mother, she had just had a baby girl named Beatrice, who for some reason was always called Mama Lucy. Louis was expected to help out with the baby. Although Mayann was jolly and good fun, she was not always responsible. She would sometimes disappear for days at a time, leaving Louis to take care of little Mama Lucy. Even though he was very young, Louis always managed to find a relative or a neighbor to help until Mayann returned.

A formal portrait of Louis, his mother, and his sister Beatrice. This photograph was taken after Armstrong began earning money as a musician and could afford not only to have the photograph taken, but to buy good clothes for himself and his family.

Despite her irresponsibility, Louis and his mother were close. Louis later said that one of the few times in his life that he cried was at his mother's funeral.

Louis Armstrong, like many kids, had his nicknames. His first one was Dippermouth, because he supposedly had a mouth as big as a dipper. (It was not that his mouth was so big, but that his wide smile made it seem so.) Later on in life some people started calling him Satchelmouth, which got shortened to Satchmo, or just Satch. (A satchel is a small suitcase.) As he became well known, musicians started calling him Pops, and often did until the end of his life. His mother called him Louis, which was what he always preferred. But most of the people who knew him, including many fans, called him Louie, the most common nickname for Louis. Louie was what his friends called him when he was a boy.

Life was not easy for this little family. Mayann washed clothes and did other kinds of odd jobs, mostly in the homes of white people, to earn what she could. Louis also worked at whatever he could to earn a few nickels and dimes. For awhile he sold newspapers on the street. He ran errands for neighbors. He helped his mother deliver laundry.

They lived on the simplest kind of food. For dinner they often had red beans and rice. Louis became very fond of this dish. Later in life he would sometimes sign his letters "Red beans and ricely yours." Other times they ate stew made of the heads of fish, which were very cheap. One of Mayann's boyfriends worked in a hotel. Often he brought home leftovers from people's dinners at the hotel restaurant. And when things were really bad, Louis would scrounge through garbage cans to see what he could find. Treats, like cookies and cake, much less ice cream, were rare in Louis Armstrong's home.

Hard as things were, all his life Louis was the sort of person who made the best of whatever was handed him, and who always saw the bright side of life. There were a lot of things for kids to do in New Orleans. The city bordered on Lake Pontchartrain, a lake big enough for excursion boats. Out by the lake there were parks— separate ones for blacks and whites. On Sundays, groups of people would go out to these parks for picnics. There would be plenty of food and drink and, naturally, a band. Louis often went out to one of the parks to hear the music, play with other kids, and ask for food from the picnickers.

There was always plenty of excitement in his own neighborhood. It was a tough place, perhaps the toughest place in the city. On practically every corner there was a "honky-tonk," that is, a saloon with one room for dancing and another room for gambling. It was an entertainment district, a "good-time" area, as people said.

Most of the customers who came into the neighborhood looking for fun were poor working men—stevedores, sailors, and men from the cotton fields, saw mills, or railroads—out to spend their small pay. They were strong and tough, and there were often fights. Occasionally there were murders.

Mixed in with the working people were the hustlers. When these gamblers, thieves, and other kinds of criminals had money, they dressed in fancy shirts, jackets, and highly polished shoes. When they were out

Anderson's was a very popular retaurant and dance hall. Many of the pioneering New Orleans jazz musicians played there at the time Armstrong was growing up. Armstrong worked at Anderson's a few times, but most of his work in the early days was in rough honky-tonks.

of money they sold their elegant clothes at pawnshops and looked for ways, legal or illegal, to get money again.

One such man who later helped Louis to become a musician was a rough character called Black Benny Williams. Black Benny played the bass drum, but he was mostly known for his hustling. Once, when Black Benny had some money, he got his good suit out of the pawnshop. He was strutting down a street in Armstrong's district when a policeman came along with a warrant for his arrest. Black Benny told the policeman, "Well, I played cards last night, and I won enough to get this suit out of pawn. Ain't been dressed up for a year." The policeman told Benny that that was too bad. He was under arrest. He grabbed Benny by the belt from behind. Benny said, "Now you can suit yourself, I ain't going to jail today." And he started marching off down the street, dragging the policeman along behind him, until finally the policeman gave up.

That was the kind of neighborhood Louis Armstrong grew up in. The two most admired kinds of people living there were the hustlers and the musicians. Louis Armstrong loved music. But how could a poor boy who could hardly afford food, much less a musical instrument, study music? For him, becoming a hustler seemed the most likely path.

Chapter 2

THE MUSIC APPRENTICE

B UT FATE TOOK OVER. ONE OF THE most famous stories in jazz history was how Louis Armstrong was sent to the Colored Waif's Home. It was customary in New Orleans for people to celebrate New Year's Eve by making a lot of noise. According to this legend, on New Year's Eve 1912 Louis wanted to make his share of noise. He knew that one of his mother's boyfriends had left a .38 pistol in their home.

Armstrong (left) and Joe "King" Oliver in a formal portrait taken in Chicago when Armstrong was with the Oliver Creole Jazz Band. Oliver was fond of Louis and acted like a substitute father to him.

Louis loaded the pistol with blank cartridges and went out to join a gang of friends. During the celebrations he fired the gun. A passing police officer quickly collared him. He was brought before a judge, who sentenced him to the Colored Waif's Home. It was at the Waif's Home that Louis learned to play the cornet.

That is the legend. The truth, as always, is more complicated. A good many years after Armstrong's death, a New Orleans researcher discovered that Louis had been in trouble with the law before. This is hardly surprising. He was desperately poor, often left to take care of his little sister when he was just a child himself. He might well have been tempted to steal, perhaps shoplifting food when he was hungry. In any case, the judge decided that Louis would be better off in the Waif's Home.

The judge was right about that, for Louis might well have turned to a career in crime if he hadn't found music. There were places like the Waif's Home in many American cities. In those days there were thousands of children, some as young as eight and ten, running in street gangs. Many of them were homeless. They slept where they could and begged, or stole, food.

New Orleans was no different. When Louis was still a small boy an African American named Joseph Jones, a former soldier, started a home for homeless black children.

He struggled for money, and eventually the city of New Orleans started paying him to take in juvenile law-breakers like Louis.

The Jones Home, as everybody called it, was run like an army camp. The boys drilled with wooden guns, scrubbed their dorms and themselves regularly, and ate the cheapest kind of food. Beans and molasses was dinner sometimes. The boys were also taught reading, writing, and arithmetic. Running the home was always difficult for Jones. He often spent his own money for food. But he didn't give up and came to be considered one of the greatest African-American leaders in New Orleans of his time.

The famous Waif's Home in New Orleans at the time Armstrong was living there. Joseph Jones, who struggled heroically to keep the Waif's Home going, is shown at the right.

At first, Louis was homesick at the Jones Home. Louis could be shy. Later, he told a story about himself involving the daughter of one of his schoolteachers. "I was in love with Wilhelmina . . . she was so kind and sweet that she had loads of admirers. I had an inferiority complex and felt that I was not good enough for her."

This shyness was undoubtedly one reason why Louis was unhappy when he was sent to the Jones Home. But he soon came to feel comfortable there. For the first time in his life he had regular meals without having to worry about them, shoes on his feet, and clean clothes. Most important, like most such places, the Jones Home had a band.

Actually, the band was not Armstrong's first venture into music. Children growing up in New Orleans took music for granted. It was everywhere around them. When he was about twelve, he belonged to a vocal quartet that sang on street corners for pennies, one of many such groups in America. Quartets of this kind sing in harmony. Louis and the others did not know how to read music, nor had they any music to read. They had to find the right harmony notes to each song by ear. According to Armstrong, he became quite good at finding the right notes. He had a very good natural ear, and the experience of singing in the vocal quartet was excellent training for it.

The band at the Jones Home was a brass band, a type very common in that day. It had drums to set the rhythms, but the other instruments were all brasses such as cornets, trombones, and alto and baritone horns.

Armstrong started in the band on drums and then moved to the alto horn. The alto horn plays much the same as the cornet, but it is slightly larger and lower in sound. The music teacher who ran the band quickly realized that Armstrong had talent. When the Home's bugler left, Armstrong took over the job, blowing various bugle calls to signal time to wake up in the

The Waif's Home band. The instruments were almost all brass winds— cornets, trombones, alto and baritone horns, as well as drums. "Little Louis" is in the top row with the arrow pointing to him.

morning, to eat meals, to work and play. The bugle is virtually the same as the cornet, except that it has no valves and plays fewer notes. On the alto horn and the bugle Louis was developing his *embouchure*. The term comes from the French word for mouth, and refers to the way the lips are placed on the mouthpiece to make sounds. Soon enough he was ready to play the cornet. (The cornet is the same as the trumpet, except that it is constructed a little differently to make it sound more mellow, while the trumpet is more brilliant sounding.)

Unfortunately Louis was not learning to form his embouchure correctly. To put it simply, he was not placing the mouthpiece exactly where he should have. Worse, he was using too much pressure. He was pushing the mouthpiece too hard against his lips. All brass players are likely to use some pressure, especially to hit high notes, but Armstrong used a lot of it. Later in life his lip would be damaged by problems with his embouchure.

Despite this, he was making progress. The Jones Home band, like many similar bands, played by ear. It is of course best for young musicians to learn to read music, and eventually Louis had to do that. But all of his ear training, first in the vocal quartet and then in the Jones Home band, was excellent practice for a

The Smithsonian National Museum in Washington, D.C., has recently acquired this old cornet, which is supposed to have been Armstrong's first cornet. Armstrong probably owned it, but it may not have been his first one.

budding jazz musician because most jazz, although not all, is played by ear.

But Louis was not only learning how to play music, he was also discovering that he loved to play it. He loved hearing melodies coming out of his cornet. He enjoyed trying to play them with a beautiful tone and filling them with expression. He would not simply play the notes correctly, but he put feeling, or meaning, into them. This ability to make his music express his feelings, to say something, would be important in attracting audiences later on.

At this time jazz was brand-new. Indeed, it was still taking form. We have no recordings of this early jazz, so much of what we believe about the beginnings of jazz is guesswork. However, we know that it was created in New Orleans and the surrounding country villages and towns by black people.

New Orleans was a complex city. It was founded by the French in the early 1700s, and for a century had little

New Orleans has always been a lively city with plenty of music and dance. This photograph, taken in the 1890s, shows a sign for the Orpheum Theater at the right. At the left is one of the many halls used for dances and other functions.

to do with the rest of America. Like most of the Caribbean islands, it got its wealth from growing cotton, rice, sugar, and other crops. Black slaves did most of the work, not only in the fields, but in the cities, too.

New Orleans had a large African-American population. But besides the blacks and whites, there was an in-between group of people who were a mixture of both. They are usually called Creoles.

The blacks and the Creoles had their own type of music. This music was a mix of the popular and dance music of whites, with the old music from Africa the black slaves had brought with them to the New World. The rhythm of African music was quite complex. The music the black people created in the American South had a bright, swinging rhythm—not the same as African rhythm, but related to it.

Out of this African-American music grew several other types of music—spirituals like "Go Down Moses," plantation songs like "Camptown Races," and the blues. Yet another form to grow out of African-American music was ragtime, which had a "ragged," bouncy beat. By 1900 ragtime was popular all over the United States with white people as well as blacks. At the time Louis Armstrong was growing up, ragtime was being transformed into jazz in New Orleans.

It is difficult for even trained musicians to explain the difference between ragtime and jazz. The difference is mainly in the rhythm. In jazz the rhythm is "looser." It swings a little more.

Nobody is sure exactly who the first jazz musicians were. A lot of them were Creoles. Some of the best known of the early jazz players, like pianist Jelly Roll Morton, trombonist Kid Ory, and clarinetist Sidney Bechet, were Creoles. But they were not alone. Other blacks had a hand in developing jazz, and soon whites were playing the music, too.

Jelly Roll Morton and his Red Hot Peppers. This band was formed in the North, although most of the musicians were from New Orleans. It was, and is, considered one of the greatest of the New Orleans style jazz bands. Pianist Morton was a flamboyant character, who boasted a lot, but he was one of the best of the early jazz musicians. Armstrong knew him, but did not work in his bands.

Louis Armstrong got out of the Jones Home in 1914. Apparently his father, who wanted him to help around his home, arranged for Louis to be released. He stayed with his father for a few months and then moved back in with his mother, where he was much happier. Once again we do not know exactly how and when Louis learned how to play the new jazz music. Many different types of bands were playing it. Some of them were parade bands with perhaps a dozen instruments, much like the brass band of the Jones Home, except that they had clarinets. Bands meant for dancing were smaller and usually consisted of cornet, trombone, clarinet, drums, and some combination of bass, guitar, and violin. Probably Louis first began playing jazz with the very rough duos and trios in the honky-tonks around his neighborhood.

At first it was a struggle for him to learn. He couldn't take the cornet from the Jones Home when he left, and he didn't have enough money to buy one for himself, even though a used instrument might cost only five dollars or so at the time. But he was determined to become a musician, and night after night he went around to the honky-tonks and begged to be allowed to sit in with the band. Sometimes the cornet player would let him. Of course, Louis would have to borrow the instrument. These bands worked long hours, and the musicians were usually happy to take a short break.

One person who helped was the tough hustler Black Benny. He took a liking to Louis and sometimes went with him to where a band was playing. If Black Benny told the leader to let Louis sit in, the leader would not dare to argue. Slowly Louis began to improve. He learned the tunes then popular around New Orleans and developed his ability to "get around" on his horn quickly. But without his own cornet to practice with, his progress was slow.

The New Orleans musicians were poorly paid. Most of them had to have day jobs as well. Louis worked at many different kinds of jobs. A lot of the time he delivered coal, which people then burned for heat and cooking. He would drive a mule cart around the city, shoveling coal out for whoever wanted it. This was hard work. Louis earned five dollars a week from his coal cart.

Finally he got enough money to buy a cornet of his own. Now he could practice regularly, and he began to move ahead. His name started to get around among musicians. He was known as a kid who had some promise.

One of the musicians who saw Louis's promise was Joe Oliver. Oliver was the cornetist with Kid Ory's band,

considered the best jazz band in New Orleans in the years around 1916 to 1919, when Louis was learning to play. Joe Oliver was a big, tough man, with a huge appetite. He would eat a whole chicken at a meal and

King Oliver was a heavy eater, but drank little alcohol. He was a big man, and tough. For awhile in the 1920s his Creole Jazz Band was considered the best of all American jazz groups. But times changed, and Oliver's band went out of fashion. He died poor in 1938.

follow it with a whole pie and a pot of coffee. Later, when Oliver had his own band, he wanted everybody to follow his orders. When he thumped his foot down on the bandstand, the band was supposed to stop playing at the end of the chorus. Once the band was having such a good time that the musicians romped on into another chorus after Joe stomped his foot. The next day he brought a brick to the bandstand. Instead of stomping his foot, he slammed the brick down. The musicians got the message.

Joe saw Louis's promise and took him under his wing. Louis was happy to take advice from Joe. Many times he would go around to Oliver's house for a meal, where Joe would explain things about music to him. Sometimes Joe would take Louis to his job and let him sit in for a number or two.

By now Louis was about sixteen. He was playing regularly in the honky-tonks as well as sitting in for Oliver in the Ory band and elsewhere. Jazz was spreading out from New Orleans. People who came to New Orleans on business or as tourists heard the new music and talked about it when they got home. (We must keep in mind that there was still no radio, and no jazz was being recorded. The only way news of it could spread was by word of mouth.) People in other cities grew curious. By 1915 there were several New Orleans jazz bands playing in dance halls and clubs in Chicago, Los Angeles, San Francisco, and a few other places.

Then in 1917 one New Orleans group, called the Original Dixieland Jazz Band, was invited to play at an important New York City restaurant. The band attracted a lot of attention and then made some records. The records of the Original Dixieland Jazz Band became hits. Soon all of America had heard about jazz.

Naturally, record companies and club owners looked for more New Orleans jazz musicians. In 1918 Joe Oliver, now called King Oliver, left New Orleans for Chicago, where the pay was much better and African Americans were not pressed down quite as hard as they were in the South. He suggested to Ory that Ory hire Louis Armstrong to play cornet. Ory said later,

There were many good, experienced trumpet players in town, but none of them had young Louis's possibilities. I went to see him and told him that if he got himself a pair of long trousers, I'd give him a job. Within two hours Louis came to my house and said, 'Here I am. I'll be glad when eight o'clock comes. I'm ready to go.'

Louis was now with the top jazz band in New Orleans. Soon, however, Ory himself left New Orleans

The Original Dixieland Jazz Band—the band that made jazz famous in America. Several other jazz bands were playing in northern cities, but the Dixieland had the luck to open in an important New York City club, where it attracted a lot of attention.

for a better-paying job in Los Angeles. Armstrong formed his own band with a friend. More importantly, in 1918, he got a job playing in a band on one of the famous Mississippi River steamboats. These boats traveled up and down the river from town to town, putting on dances. The bands played from written music and were strictly disciplined. Now Louis had to improve his reading and learn to play just the way the leader wanted him to. It was good training for him. On the riverboats Louis became a more polished musician.

He was now a grown man and a professional musician. But he was still in New Orleans, while a lot of his friends had gone elsewhere to make names for themselves. Louis himself had been offered jobs in the North and on the West Coast. But he was shy and not ready to leave the familiar places of his hometown. So he stayed.

Up in Chicago, King Oliver was leading one of the best-known jazz bands in the city. In 1922 he decided he wanted a second cornetist in the band so he could rest his lip from time to time. He sent a telegram to Louis. This time Louis decided to go. He knew if he was under the wing of Oliver, he could rest easy. So Louis got on a train, carrying the cornet, a small suitcase, and a fish sandwich Mayann made for him, and headed for Chicago and fame.

Chapter 3

GREATNESS

IN THE 1920s CHICAGO WAS FAMOUS FOR its rough edges and its roaring good times. The city was full of clubs and dance halls. Most of them were owned by gangsters who did not hesitate to murder their rivals. Many of the politicians who ran the city were corrupt and took bribes from the gangsters to let them do what they wanted to.

It was, like many American cities, a town of immigrants. Newly arrived Poles, Bohemians, Jews, and many others, speaking their own languages

A photo of Armstrong about the time he was beginning to record under his own name. It was probably made for publicity purposes.

and following their own folkways, made a patchwork quilt of the city. There were also many African Americans coming in to escape the poverty and harshness of the South. There was a lot of poverty in Chicago, too, and a lot of hard work, but there were good times as well.

It was a great city for a young jazz musician. There were plenty of jobs for musicians who could play music for dancing. Everybody knew that the best musicians were from New Orleans, although northern players, both black and white, were catching up.

King Oliver's Creole Jazz Band was playing at the Lincoln Gardens, a big dance hall with fake leaves on the ceiling. Oliver specialized in the plunger mute, with which he would make his cornet cry like a baby. Lincoln Gardens was mainly for blacks, but young white teenagers who wanted to become jazz musicians often went there to hear Oliver's band.

Louis was expected to play a quiet second part to King Oliver's cornet lead, which suited Louis most of the time. But when Oliver wanted to rest his lip, Louis would step out of the shadows and take the lead. Although Louis was sometimes quiet with people, his playing was always strong and dramatic. Once he put the cornet to his lips his shyness disappeared.

We can hear this boldness in his first records. In 1923 the Creole Jazz Band recorded a series of records that are still considered very important by jazz critics. There are not many solos on these records, but Armstrong has one on a tune called "Froggie Moore." When his solo starts the music suddenly becomes brighter. Armstrong is playing with a livelier swing than the others. Most important, he shows the inventiveness that would be evident in his great records. Louis had an ability to make up fresh and exciting musical phrases that surpassed all other jazz musicians. This showed in his "Froggie Moore" solo.

A publicity photo of the Oliver Creole Jazz Band. Jazz was sometimes publicized as a humorous music, and the musicians are making comic poses. Armstrong is kneeling in front, posing with a slide cornet, which he rarely played. Oliver is just behind him, holding a plunger mute to the bell of his cornet. Lil Hardin, soon to marry Louis, is at the piano.

Lil and Louis clowning around for a photograph, taken in Hollywood in 1930. By this time Armstrong was moving into the big time, playing top clubs and making hit records.

The pianist in the Creole Jazz Band was a young woman named Lillian Hardin. She had had some musical training and knew more about music theory than most of the others. She was soon attracted to Louis. She believed he needed to get over his shyness and let his great talent shine through. Louis was overweight and Lil put him on a diet. She made him buy fashionable new clothes and get a stylish haircut. Finally, she married him.

Lil was determined that her husband should not play second cornet behind Oliver for very long. As it happened, a New York bandleader named Fletcher Henderson had once heard Armstrong in New Orleans. He had been impressed. By 1924 Henderson's band was becoming well known around New York. It was not, however, a typical small New Orleans jazz band playing by ear.

The fashion in popular music was changing. The public wanted larger bands playing interesting arrangements to dance to. The Fletcher Henderson Orchestra had ten or eleven pieces. It was not as hot as the New Orleans bands playing around Chicago, but its members could all read music well and could play the tricky arrangements the band featured.

Fletcher Henderson had heard from other musicians that Armstrong was now in Chicago and playing better than ever. He offered Louis a job. The idea of leaving Oliver made Louis very nervous. He was so nervous that he was afraid to tell Oliver the news. However, Lil insisted that Louis go to New York. Chicago may have been roaring, but New York City was the center of American show business. Most of the big record companies, music publishers, and booking offices were there.

So Armstrong went to New York to join Fletcher Henderson. The men in the band were very proud of their musicianship. They dressed in the latest style and owned big, expensive cars. They made Louis shyer than ever. He later said, "I had just left Chicago, where the way we used to do it was just take the wind in, and . . . blow it out—now I got to watch this part [the written music]. I was pretty stiff, so they didn't know whether I could play or not. After two weeks I still hadn't even stretched." His shyness was holding him back.

Then a clarinet player named Buster Bailey, whom Louis had known in Chicago, joined the band. Having a friend around made him more comfortable. Louis remembered, "They jumped on 'Tiger Rag,' I think it was, and they gave me about four choruses—following Buster Bailey made me really come on a little bit."

From that point on Louis Armstrong was the jazz star of the band. He made many brilliant solos with the

The Fletcher Henderson Orchestra, one of the best hot dance bands of the 1920s. Armstrong is in the center of the back row. Henderson is at the piano. The saxophonist at left is Coleman Hawkins, rapidly becoming known as the leading saxophonist in jazz.

orchestra. Especially fine were the ones on "Shanghai Shuffle," "Bye and Bye," and "Money Blues." The standout, however, was "Sugarfoot Stomp." This was really "Dippermouth Blues," a tune on which King Oliver played a famous solo still imitated by musicians today, but now Armstrong played the solo his own way. Louis had outdistanced his teacher.

Louis Armstrong only stayed with the Fletcher Henderson Orchestra for a year. During that time he also made some freelance records with "pick-up" groups put together for the records. On one of these he accompanies the great blues singer Bessie Smith in the classic song, "St. Louis Blues." "Everybody Loves My Baby," made with the Clarence Williams' Blue Five, is another example of his great inventive ability. Perhaps more than anything, Armstrong was able to improvise solos made up of phrases that seemed to belong together. It is one thing to do this when you sit down at the piano and work out a song. It is another to do it on the spur of the moment standing in front of an audience. In his solo on "Everybody Loves My Baby" Armstrong plays a little four-note figure again and again, but varies it a little each time. In his solos Armstrong was not just swinging. He was building complete musical structures.

Louis Armstrong did not become well known to the public during his stint with the Henderson Orchestra. But the young jazz musicians around New York began to hear about him. They listened to all his solos on records and crowded around to hear him in person when they could. (Most of the clubs and ballrooms where the Henderson Orchestra played were for whites only. Black musicians could not get in to such places unless they were in the band, but sometimes they could listen from behind the bandstand.) Rex Stewart, later a star cornet player with the Duke Ellington Orchestra, said, "Then Louis Armstrong hit town! I went mad with the rest of the town. I tried to walk like him, talk like him, eat like him, sleep like him. I even bought a big pair of policeman shoes like he used to wear and stood outside of his apartment waiting for him to come out so I could look at him." Many other musicians said the same. In the jazz world, Louis was becoming an important person.

Louis had always liked to sing, although his voice was somewhat rough. After he had been with Fletcher Henderson for awhile, he begged the leader to let him sing. Henderson wondered what Louis could possibly sing with his rough voice, but reluctantly he let Louis sing the fast, rollicking "Everybody Loves My Baby." "He was great," Henderson said. "The band loved it, and the crowds just ate it up." It was the start of a career that would make Louis Armstrong one of the most famous singers in the world.

But Louis was not entirely happy with the Henderson Orchestra. He had only a few solos a night.

Often the band had to play ordinary sentimental tunes the dancers wanted. Despite his shyness, Louis wanted to be out front more, playing jazz. Besides, his wife, Lil, was living in Chicago. She urged him to come back and start his own orchestra.

So in the fall of 1925, he went back to Chicago. And almost immediately he began to record a series of records under his own name, considered to be among the greatest of all jazz records ever made.

It was probably Lil's idea for Louis to record under his own name, but already record producers knew about his growing reputation. The OKeh Record Company decided to take a chance on Louis. In November 1925 he cut the first of this series. They were issued under several names, but many were titled *Louis Armstrong and His Hot Five*. The series is usually known as the *Hot Fives*.

During this period, around 1926, Louis switched from cornet to trumpet. We are not exactly sure when he made the switch. The instruments sound so much alike it is hard to tell from the old recordings. But by 1927 he was mainly playing trumpet.

These early records were ten inches in diameter and turned at seventy-eight revolutions per minute. The musicians gathered around a huge cone-shaped horn, which took in the music and recorded it on a wax surface. Yet despite the primitive setup, the sound was surprisingly good. Within the next year electrical recording, using microphones, was introduced. Recording techniques improved.

Armstrong's Hot Five was only a recording group. The personnel shifted. This early version shows Louis at the piano, with his wife, Lil, at the right.

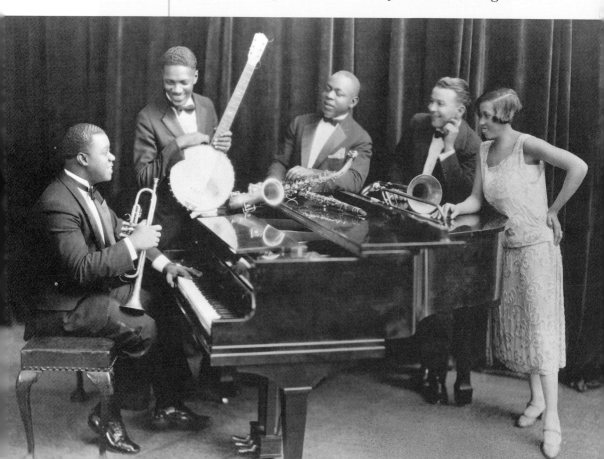

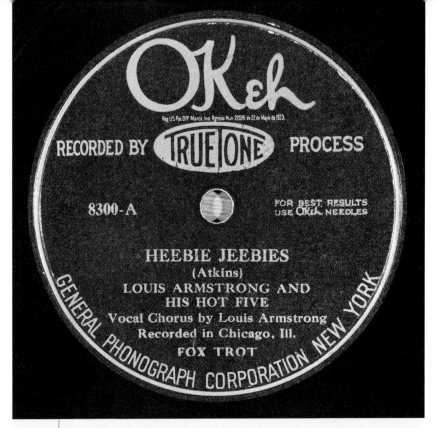

OKeh's record, the Heebie Jeebies

Today, even with many technicians working, it may take months to make a recording. In the 1920s a handful of musicians went into a studio for a few hours, cut two to eight sides, collected fifty dollars a man, and went off to play their regular jobs. This is how the *Hot Fives* were made. Some of the tunes were ordinary popular songs, some were written by Lil, Louis, or members of the band. The arrangements were worked out in brief rehearsals in Lil's living room or in the studio. It was all done very quickly.

There are so many masterpieces in the *Hot Five* series that it is hard to single any out. "Cornet Chop Suey" and "Potato Head Blues" feature Armstrong playing stop-time solos. In these solos the band played just one note every one or two measures, leaving Louis free to invent as he wished. "Heebie Jeebies" features Louis in what was called a "scat" vocal, that is, singing nonsense words to the tune. And "Hotter Than That" is indeed one of the hottest solos on the records.

But nearly everyone agrees that the masterpiece of the series was one of the last ones, made in 1928 called "West End Blues." It begins with a long, astonishing, unaccompanied introduction by Louis, followed by a mournful playing of the main melody to the tune. Some other members of the band solo, and then Louis takes a closing solo. This opens with a long note, followed by a series of swirling, scurrying figures, and then a quiet ending. Like the finest of Armstrong's solos, it makes sense, like a dramatic play or novel. Many critics consider it the greatest of all jazz recordings and it is less than three minutes long.

With the *Hot Five* series, people now began to realize that jazz was not just a lively music to dance to, but could be considered a form of art. Louis Armstrong was still not widely known to the public, but among jazz musicians and jazz fans he was now the star.

Louis ARMSTRONG Plays Selmer TRUMPET Exclusively

Chapter 4

THE POPULAR BAND LEADER

The Chicago where Armstrong was living roared louder than ever. The gangsters did what they pleased. They had their own doctors and lawyers. They even had their own hospital where they could go when they had been wounded in a gun battle.

The South Side entertainment district, where there were many clubs and dance halls, was particularly tough. Earl Hines, Louis's pianist, said, "It was lit up at night like Paris, and there were some of the most dangerous people in the world on it. . . . Somebody was always getting hurt, and you

Armstrong in a publicity photograph for Selmer, the company that supplied Louis with his trumpets.

had to have a certain amount of courage to work in those clubs."

One of the toughest people there was Tack Annie. Once, when she got rowdy in a club, it took four policemen to get her out. Armstrong himself was occasionally threatened. One time a gangster started beating up his own girlfriend on the dance floor in front of everybody. When he saw Louis watching him he walked over, waved his pistol at Louis, and asked him if he had any objections. All Louis could say was, "That's all right with me."

But if Chicago was rough, it was also a great place for musicians. There was no recorded music in public places. Every little club, restaurant, and bar had at least a pianist. Many of them had full bands. In those days people were dance-crazy and would get up to dance right in the middle of their meal at a restaurant.

Times were particularly good for African-American entertainers. It was becoming fashionable for white people to go to black clubs and dance halls to enjoy black singers, musicians, dancers, and comedians. Soon owners of white restaurants and clubs were hiring black musicians to play for white audiences. By the mid-1920s Armstrong could make seventy-five dollars a week, which was very good pay for that time.

Jazz was now being played for all Americans—rich and poor, black and white.

By about 1927 the new type of dance music, using larger orchestras playing from arrangements, was taking over. The people who came to the clubs and theaters where Armstrong was playing wanted this kind of music. Although Louis was making recordings in the old small-band New Orleans style, in the clubs he was playing with larger groups. Of course the musicians made the music swing and left plenty of room for solos, but it was no longer the type of music that had come out of New Orleans.

Louis Armstrong and his orchestra in 1929, when he was beginning to rise to stardom.

Louis didn't mind. He liked being in front of the orchestra playing his solos. He sang more frequently. The people in the clubs enjoyed his singing, even if his voice was rough. Besides the singing, he frequently told jokes and did comedy. Through these years Louis Armstrong was becoming more of an all-around entertainer.

But the glory years of the Chicago jazz scene were about to end. Ordinary people from Chicago were getting tired of murder, robbery, and the rattle of machine guns. In an election in 1928 they voted out the old, corrupt government that was allowing the gangsters to do what they pleased. Many of the clubs where the jazz musicians had been working were illegal. The new government closed them. The good times for musicians in Chicago were over.

Fortunately for Louis, he now had a manager. This was a young white man named Tommy Rockwell. He worked for OKeh, Armstrong's record company. He also had gangster connections. He was interested in promoting black entertainers and signed Louis to a contract.

Rockwell believed that Louis could become very popular with the general public. But he knew that while the jazz fans loved to hear Armstrong play

"Hotter Than That" and "West End Blues," ordinary dancers wanted to hear the popular songs of the day. Tommy Rockwell put together a band for Louis and had arrangements made of pop songs like "I Can't Give You Anything But Love" for Louis. Now Louis would sing on almost every recording. He was happy to do that. He liked singing, and he liked pop songs. For the rest of his life he would sing them.

Louis was starting a new career. Unfortunately it soon brought him trouble. Louis, we must remember, did not have much schooling. He was naturally smart and a musical genius, but in business he was sometimes lost. Unhappily, while he was working with Rockwell, he also signed a contract with John Collins, another very tough, hard-drinking man. Collins was connected to some gangsters in Chicago, while Rockwell had ties to gangsters in New York. Both sets of gangsters wanted Louis to play in clubs they owned. They began to fight over him.

One night a gangster crashed into Louis's dressing room in Chicago. He told Louis that he was to start playing at a club in New York the following night. Louis said:

I tell him I got this Chicago engagement and don't plan no traveling. And I turn my back on him to show I'm so cool. Then I hear this sound: SNAP! CLICK! *I turn around and he has pulled this vast revolver on me and cocked it. So I look down at that steel and say, 'Weeelllll, maybe I* do *open in New York tomorrow.'*

As soon as the gangster left, Louis told John Collins about it. Collins told Louis to hide in a phone booth below the glass. Then he got the band out of the club. But instead of sending the men to New York, he shipped them to Louisville, Kentucky. He slipped Louis out of the club and sent him to Louisville, too. The famous Kentucky Derby horse race was on, and there were many tourists there for the race. Collins was able to get the band a job. Unfortunately this squabbling between the gangsters over rights to Armstrong meant that for the next two or three years he had to stay away from both New York and Chicago as much as possible. He lost out on good jobs and the publicity he might have got from playing in New York. Later Armstrong said, "Oh, danger was dancing all around you back then."

With all these problems, Collins started looking around for other places for Louis to play. By the early

1930s some people in Europe, especially England and France, had learned about American jazz and were eager to hear more of it. The audience for jazz in Europe was not large, but it was enthusiastic. Collins let jazz fans in England know that Louis might come over. They quickly arranged for him to play at a famous London theater, the Palladium.

So off went Louis and Collins. The lazy Collins had not arranged for any other gigs, nor had he hired a band to play with Armstrong. There was no planning. Nonetheless, a band was hastily organized. Jazz fans packed the Palladium night after night for two weeks. Some people came every night for the whole time Louis was there.

Armstrong with a pick-up orchestra, probably in Paris. Louis's European tours were usually very successful. Europeans had not heard much jazz and liked the novelty of it, although there were few serious fans.

After that John Collins was able to arrange a few one-nighters, but mostly Louis relaxed. He needed the rest. He had been playing so much for so many years that his lip was not only tired, but it bled some-times when he was playing. The problems were both overwork and his poor embouchure. He was using too much pressure. Bit by bit his lip was being damaged.

The trip to England was important for Louis, for it made him known in Europe. In 1933 he made another trip to England, which ended with a tour of several European countries, including France, Denmark, and Holland. However Collins managed the tour badly, and Louis was finally fed up with him. He fired him when the European tour ended and did without a manager for awhile. But most entertainers needed managers, especially African Americans who had to have somebody to represent them to the whites who ran the theaters, clubs, and record companies. This was par-ticularly the case in the 1930s. The Great Depression had fallen like a shadow across America. Millions were out of work, families were losing their homes, children were going to bed hungry. These were hard times.

Then Louis ran into a man he had known from his Chicago days. His name was Joe Glaser, and like many others, he was having a hard time. He decided that there

Armstrong in 1937 with his manager Joe Glaser (left) and Cork O'Keefe (right), a highly respected band booker and music business professional. Glaser was a tough manager who was important in making Louis a star.

was a good opportunity for him in representing black talent. He wanted to manage Louis Armstrong. Glaser was tough and swore a lot, but performers learned that they could trust Joe Glaser's word.

So Louis and Joe teamed up. It is probably true that Joe Glaser took a larger share of Louis's earnings than he should have. But Glaser was determined to make Louis Armstrong a big star. Now Louis had a good manager who saw to it that things went right. He had plenty of jobs for good pay. He also began to appear in movies. Louis became the first African-American entertainer to appear regularly on a sponsored radio show. He sang and played in a Broadway show called *Swingin' the Dream*. By 1940 Louis was a popular music star.

Some jazz fans complained that Armstrong was playing too many pop tunes and not as much jazz as they wanted to hear. Louis heard these complaints, but they did not much bother him. He was a great jazz musician, true, but he was also an entertainer.

Armstrong playing in the famous Colosseum in Rome in a gag photograph for publicity purposes.

He felt it was his job to make his audiences happy and give them the kind of popular songs they liked.

Although Armstrong was now more interested in pleasing his audiences than in playing great jazz, he could not help making many wonderful solos. Among the best from this time are his solos on recordings of "Star Dust," "Mahogany Hall Stomp," "Ev'ntide," and "Struttin' with Some Barbecue." Especially interesting is his second solo in "Sweethearts on Parade." In this solo he alternates sections of quiet, somewhat sweet passages, with rapid, chattering, double-time tense ones. Once again we see Armstrong's ability to give shape to his solos in a way that most jazz improvisers do not.

Louis was now a star, but the good times would not last. During the 1930s and into the 1940s the swing music of the big dance bands like Armstrong's were very popular in the United States. They played a mixture of jazz and ordinary dance music that the public loved. Then, in 1941, the United States got into World War II. Many musicians went into the army and navy. Gas, tires, and many other things were needed for the war, and bands found it hard to travel. By the end of the war many of the big dance bands were in trouble.

A still photograph from a movie called "Artists and Models." During the late 1930s Armstrong appeared in a movie almost every year. He made many more later in his career.

Worse was to come. By the end of the war in 1946, the American people had had fifteen years of depression and war. They wanted peace and quiet. They were no longer interested in exciting swing music. They turned to smooth-voiced singers of romantic songs, like Frank Sinatra and Perry Como. Very quickly the swing bands collapsed. With them went Louis Armstrong. After twenty years of fame and good fortune, he was being forgotten.

Chapter 5

THE INTERNATIONAL STAR

JOE GLASER SAW THE SWING BANDS dying and wondered what to do about Louis. Starting with Armstrong, he had built up a stable of African-American singers and musicians. He was now very successful and a power in the entertainment industry.

Joe and Louis had not become best friends, but they respected each other. Joe Glaser knew that Louis had given him his start in the music business. Joe felt a lot of loyalty to Louis. He would try to do something for him.

Armstrong in a publicity shot from the 1940s. He was grinning, but business was not good.

He looked around. At the time there was a revival of interest in the old New Orleans music that Louis had started out playing. It was now called Dixieland. It was not as popular as the swing music of the big dance bands had been, but it had quite a large following of fans. Some of Louis's old friends from New Orleans, like Sidney Bechet, were gaining greater fame than they had ever had.

In 1947 Louis appeared in the movie *New Orleans*, playing in a Dixieland band. At about the same time, he gave some concerts with Dixieland bands. The movie brought him a lot of publicity, and the concerts, too, were successful. Joe Glaser realized that this might be Louis's chance. New Orleans jazz was coming back, and Louis was the greatest of all the New Orleans musicians. Also singers were popular, and Louis was a singer. Quickly Glaser organized a Dixieland band for Louis, which was called the All Stars. And indeed they were, for it included pianist Earl Hines and trombonist Jack Teagarden, two of the best improvisers in jazz history.

Still, would the public like it? The band opened in Los Angeles in August 1947. Many stars of pop music turned out at the opening. *Time* magazine carried a story about the Armstrong All Stars. The public loved the band. By 1949 *Down Beat* magazine said that the

All Stars were "probably the highest paid unit of its size in existence." That same year Louis was on the cover of *Time*.

Through the next years his fame continued to grow. Jazz critics and jazz fans were not always happy with the music. Louis was doing more singing than trumpet playing. While his singing was always enjoyable, jazz people wanted to hear Louis play great jazz solos on the trumpet.

As usual, Louis ignored these complaints. For one thing, his problems with his lip had gradually grown worse. His upper lip was now a mass of scar tissue, as can be seen from any photograph taken of him at this time.

The great success of the All Stars brought Armstrong even greater fame than before, as this photo of him on the cover of Time *magazine suggests.*

A person with scarred lips will always have trouble playing a wind instrument. Louis simply had to sing a lot to rest his lip.

But the fact is that as always, what Louis wanted most of all was to please those millions of fans who bought his records and came to his concerts. Most of these people were interested in Louis, not jazz. In his singing and clowning around he always seemed warmhearted and open. People loved him for who he was.

But Louis was not willing to please his fans at all costs. During the 1950s there was much racial friction in the United States. Blacks were tired of being held back. They wanted an end to segregated schools, buses, restaurants, and movie theaters. This was especially true in the South where segregation was the law.

Armstrong and a young English fan in 1970. By this time Louis was one of the best-known entertainers in the world.

There were many demonstrations in which people got hurt. A few black leaders were even murdered for being outspoken about rights for African Americans.

In one highly publicized case, the schools of Little Rock, the capital of Arkansas, were ordered by federal courts to integrate. But when black students appeared at a white school they were greeted by an angry mob of whites, some of whom spit at the students. The governor of Arkansas said he would not allow the schools of his state to integrate, even though the court said they must.

Louis Armstrong was playing a gig in Grand Forks, North Dakota, at the time. He saw the incident on television in his dressing room. Just at that moment a young reporter from a local paper came backstage to interview Louis about his show. But instead of talking about music, Louis ripped into the United States government. He said that President Eisenhower had "no guts" for allowing this to happen and that he had no use for the government for "the way they are treating my people in the South."

The story made headlines across the United States. Louis had always been known as a cheerful, good-humored entertainer. He was not known as one who attacked people, especially the president. In fact, some

In the late 1950s schools everywhere in America were supposed to admit black students on an equal basis with whites. Many southerners objected, as did Arkansas' governor, Orval Faubus.

blacks had criticized Louis earlier for not speaking out about segregation before. But now Louis had done so, and thereafter he occasionally commented on the issue. For awhile, he even refused to play in his old hometown, New Orleans, because of the segregation laws still on the books there.

During the 1950s and 1960s Louis continued to play in public with the All Stars, but many of his hit records were made with special bands. Most of the songs he sang were ordinary romantic pop tunes, like "A Kiss to Build a Dream On," and "I Get Ideas." He had a big hit with "Blueberry Hill." He had an even bigger one with "Mack the Knife," a sort of operatic song from a musical called *The Threepenny Opera*.

Then in 1963 a musical called *Hello, Dolly* was about to open on Broadway. The producers of the movie wanted somebody well known to record the main song from the show. Somebody suggested Louis Armstrong. He recorded "Hello, Dolly." The recording began to sell quickly. By February 1964 it was on the best-seller lists. In May, it reached the number one spot, bumping out a recording by the Beatles, at the time the most famous pop group in the world. Louis Armstrong, the poor boy from New Orleans, was now at the top of the heap.

But Louis had not given up jazz altogether. He still included a lot of it in his live performances, and he made some good jazz records, like an LP called *Satch Plays Fats*, a collection of tunes by the great jazz pianist, Fats Waller. Perhaps the best of the records made during the All Star period is a set called *Satchmo: A Musical Autobiography of Louis Armstrong*. For this set Louis recorded again many of the tunes he had played at the beginning of his career. These were the ones that first made him famous, like "St. Louis Blues" and "Everybody Loves My Baby." The record producer insisted that the band come to the studio well rested, and he kept the recording sessions down to three hours. On some of these remakes, Louis played even better than he did on the original recordings. Louis Armstrong could still play great jazz.

By the 1960s he was famous not only in America but worldwide. He traveled to Europe, Africa, South America, and Japan. In fact, he was so popular that the United States government asked him to tour foreign countries as a "goodwill ambassador" of America. Some people called him "Ambassador Satch."

Louis loved to travel. He loved to play for large audiences. But he did not rest as much as he should have. He was not always careful about his diet, and he had spent countless thousands of hours playing in smoke-filled clubs and dance halls. By the late 1960s he was suffering from shortness of breath due to a heart problem. He had to sing in short bursts and grab a breath in between. He now played trumpet very little. His doctors told him he ought to retire. But to Louis the most important things were to sing and play for people. So he went on giving concerts and shows. He was planning yet one more tour when he died on July 6, 1971.

He left the world a great heritage of thousands of hours of brilliant music that people born long after he died still listen to with pleasure. Not long ago, a vocal recording of his "What a Wonderful World" was used in a movie and captured the hearts of millions of new fans. Long after he was gone, that applause was still ringing.

Armstrong poses with his fourth wife, Lucille, before the famous statue of the Sphinx in Egypt.

TIME LINE

1901 August 4: Louis Armstrong is born in New Orleans, Louisiana.

1918 Louis takes the place of Joe Oliver, his teacher and mentor, in the Kid Ory Band.

1924 February: Louis marries Lil Hardin. September: Louis moves to New York City to join the Fletcher Henderson Orchestra.

1925 November: Louis makes his first recordings as a leader with his own group, called Louis Armstrong and His Hot Five.

1932 Louis travels to London. He tours Great Britian for three months.

1935 January: Joe Glaser becomes Louis's manager.

1957 Armstrong speaks out against racial inequality. He cancels a tour of Russia in protest of school segregation in Little Rock, Arkansas.

1971 July 6: Louis Armstrong dies.

Author's Note on Sources

There are many books about Louis Armstrong. The most scholarly is *Louis Armstrong: An American Genius*, by James Lincoln Collier (Oxford: New York, 1983). *Satchmo: My Life in New Orleans* is Armstrong's autobiography of his youth (Da Capo Press: New York; orig. Prentice-Hall, 1955). *The Louis Armstrong Companion: Eight Decades of Commentary* edited by Joshua Berrett (Schimer: New York, 1999) contains a lot of material about Armstrong, including some of his own writing. *Louis Armstrong: In His Own Words*, edited by Thomas Brothers (Oxford: New York, 1999) is a collection of Armstrong's jottings and letters, mostly previously unpublished.

INDEX

ABOUT THE AUTHOR

James Lincoln Collier has written many books, both fiction and nonfiction, for children and adults. His interests span history, biography, and historical fiction. He is an authority on the history of jazz and performs weekly on the trombone in New York City.

My Brother Sam Is Dead was named a Newbery Honor Book and a Jane Addams Honor Book and was a finalist for a National Book Award. *Jump Ship to Freedom* and *War Comes to Willy Freemen* were each named a notable Children's Trade Book in the Field of Social Studies by the National Council for Social Studies and the Children's Book Council. Collier received the Christopher Award for *Decision in Philadelphia: The Constitutional Convention of 1787*. He lives in Pawling, New York.